Charles Sears Baldwin

The Expository Paragraph and Sentence

An Elementary Manual of Composition

Charles Sears Baldwin

The Expository Paragraph and Sentence
An Elementary Manual of Composition

ISBN/EAN: 9783337278106

Printed in Europe, USA, Canada, Australia, Japan

Cover: Foto ©Thomas Meinert / pixelio.de

More available books at **www.hansebooks.com**

THE EXPOSITORY PARAGRAPH AND SENTENCE

AN ELEMENTARY MANUAL OF COMPOSITION

THE EXPOSITORY
PARAGRAPH AND SENTENCE

AN ELEMENTARY MANUAL
OF COMPOSITION

BY

CHARLES SEARS BALDWIN, A.M., Ph.D.

INSTRUCTOR IN RHETORIC IN YALE UNIVERSITY

NEW YORK

LONGMANS, GREEN, AND CO.

LONDON AND BOMBAY

1898

FIRST EDITION, SEPTEMBER, 1897
REPRINTED, SEPTEMBER, 1898

Press of J. J. Little & Co.
Astor Place, New York

PREFACE

This little manual aims to supply for the first term in college such elementary instruction as seems necessary in reviewing and supplementing the work of the preparatory schools before proceeding to more special courses. To this end it deals exclusively with structure, and with expository structure as being at once more obvious, more useful, and less artistic than the other kinds. The book may thus be used as a direct introduction to Mr. Lamont's *Specimens of Exposition*, for instance, or to Mr. Brewster's *Studies in Structure and Style*. But it aspires to more general usefulness as a students' pocket-book of rhetoric.

For advice on the manuscript and for corrections in proof I am indebted to my colleague, Mr. Chauncey Wetmore Wells ; for the latter favour, to Professor Thomas R. Price and Professor G. R. Carpenter of Columbia University.

C. S. B.

YALE UNIVERSITY, *July*, 1897.

CONTENTS

vii

INTRODUCTION

Beneath all forms of prose lie four kinds of writing, which, though variously combined, are yet distinct and separate. These are *description*, the methods of suggesting mental images corresponding in some degree to scenes beheld or imagined by the writer ; *narration*, the methods of conducting a story ; *persuasion*, the methods of moving men to action, whether through their reason or through their feelings ; and *exposition*, the methods of lucid explanation. The principles set forth in this book, though they are generally applicable to all four kinds, are here applied exclusively to exposition. All brief pieces of exposition are included in the extended sense given here to the term *essay*.

The direct use of these rules of construction is confined to revision. Indirectly, sound principles, and even sound rules of detail, may lead to good habits ; but directly they are of no use till something, at least, is written. To write by rule, in the sense of pausing to apply rules in the process of composition, is, of course, futile. In that sense probably nobody ever wrote by rule. To rewrite by rule is simply to follow the method of progress in any art.

I. The Composition as a Whole.

A. The Composition Considered as a Brief Undivided Whole.

1. Composition in any art is guided by three fundamental principles : unity, coherence, emphasis. The principle of unity demands that the whole composition shall show one main purpose and have one main effect, and that every part of it shall harmonize with that purpose and contribute to that effect. Negatively, unity means the exclusion of everything irrelevant or incongruous. In writing it expresses the difference between an accumulation of notes and an essay.

2. Unity appears plainly in the following essay of Bacon :

OF ADVERSITY.

It was a high speech of Seneca (after the manner of the Stoics), *that the good things which belong to prosperity are to be wished ;*

but the good things that belong to adversity
5 *are to be admired.* *Bona rerum secundarum*
optabilia, adversarum mirabilia. Certainly
if miracles be the command over nature, they
appear most in adversity. It is yet a higher
speech of his than the other (much too high for
10 a heathen), *It is true greatness to have in one*
the frailty of a man, and the security of a
god. *Vere magnum, habere fragilitatem*
hominis, securitatem dei. This would have
done better in poesy, where transcendences [1]
15 are more allowed. And the poets, indeed,
have been busy with it ; for it is in effect the
thing which is figured in that strange fiction
of the ancient poets, which seemeth not to be
without mystery ; nay, and to have some ap-
20 proach to the state of a Christian ; that *Her-*
cules, when he went to unbind Prometheus
(by whom human nature is represented), *sailed*
the length of the great ocean in an earthen
pot or pitcher; lively describing Christian
25 resolution, that saileth in the frail bark of the
flesh through the waves of the world. But to
speak in a mean.[2] The virtue of prosperity is
temperance, the virtue of adversity is fortitude ;
which in morals [3] is the more heroical virtue.
30 Prosperity is the blessing of the Old Testa-

[1] hyperboles.   [2] *i.e.,* in plain prose.   [3] ethics.

ment; adversity is the blessing of the New, which carrieth the greater benediction, and the clearer revelation of God's favour. Yet even in the Old Testament, if you listen to David's harp, you shall hear as many hearse-like airs 35 as carols ; and the pencil of the Holy Ghost hath laboured more in describing the afflictions of Job than the felicities of Solomon. Prosperity is not without many fears and distastes ; and adversity is not without comforts and hopes. 40 We see in needleworks and embroideries, it is more pleasing to have a lively work upon a sad and solemn ground, than to have a dark and melancholy work upon a lightsome ground. Judge therefore of the pleasure of the heart by 45 the pleasure of the eye. Certainly virtue is like precious odours, most fragrant when they are incensed[1] or crushed : for prosperity doth best discover vice, but adversity doth best discover virtue.   50

3. Here is nothing that does not contribute to the elucidation of the theme—*The blessings of adversity are superior to the blessings of prosperity.* To test the unity of any brief essay, try to sum it up thus in a single

[1] burned.

sentence. And, in shaping rough notes into an essay, let the first step be to express the theme, not in a topic, as *The Uses of Translations*, but rather in a sentence, as *The use of translations is a hindrance in the acquisition of a language*, or *Some knowledge of a literature may be gained through translations*. Then, by successive modifications of this trial sentence and of the notes, bring the two into harmony.

4. The principle of coherence demands that the composition shall proceed in natural sequence without break or jar, that one thing shall lead to another. This means, of course, that the thoughts must be brought into order. It usually means also that the logical relation between each thought and the preceding shall be, not merely latent, but explicit. In the essay quoted above, the second thought is explicitly connected with the first by the correspondence of phrase : *It was a high speech —It is yet a higher speech*. The transitional phrase, *But to speak in a mean* (26), leads naturally to the following summary. But the thought, *Prosperity is not without many fears* (38), etc., is brought in abruptly. It is not

out of relation, but its relation is not shown. Most students will find it necessary to make a separate revision solely to insure the explicit reference that is so important a part of coherence.

5. The principle of emphasis demands that those parts which elucidate the theme directly shall have prominence of position and of space. Negatively, this means that whatever is merely indirect or subsidiary must be kept subordinate. Now the most prominent position in any piece of writing is the end. Thus of all laws of composition the most familiar is climax. In the essay above, Bacon closes with a pithy iteration of the theme in a sort of proverb. The reference to the Psalms (line 34) or the figure of embroidery (line 41) would make an ending obviously inferior because those parts are subsidiary. The law of emphasis, then, coincides with the law of unity in keeping uppermost in mind the conclusion.

6. Next to the end the most emphatic place is the beginning. Introduction being often unnecessary in brief essays, a direct statement of the theme, such as that which

results from the revision for unity, may often be made in the very first sentence. In any case, wherever the essay begins, with or without introduction, the theme should usually be stated there. Thus many good essays begin and end with the theme.

7. Prominence of position, however, is not more important than prominence of space. In a short essay especially, nothing of indirect bearing should receive more than a few lines. In the essay above, the illustrations from the myth of Hercules and from embroidery are the only ones stated, and these doubtless because neither would have been plain from mere allusion. Mere allusion suffices for the rest, and here appears a due proportion of space. Proportion, in fact, sums up in a word this aspect of the law of emphasis.

B. The Composition Considered as a Series of Paragraphs.

8. So soon as an essay is developed beyond a certain length, it falls naturally into paragraphs corresponding more or less to some

division of the subject into parts. A paragraph [1] is a part which, during the process of composition, has defined itself as one distinct stage in the progress of the essay. It is a unit, but a component unit. As a unit it is marked for the eye by indentation,[2] and is governed by the principles of unity, coherence, and emphasis. As a component, being like a link in a chain or a step in a stair, it contains in its first sentence some reference to the preceding paragraph.

9. By expressing the gist of each paragraph in a single sentence, one may reduce an essay to its lowest terms without affecting its coherence. By conceiving, on the other hand, each paragraph amplified into a chapter, one has a graphic idea of what is meant by the devel-

---

[1] The term paragraph is commonly applied also to what are sometimes called " isolated " or " unrelated " paragraphs. Thus a brief editorial is often called a paragraph. In this book the term is used only in the sense defined above.

[2] Since indentation is the accepted indication of a new paragraph, the student is warned never to indent except for that purpose.

opment[1] of a theme.   Bacon might easily
have presented the extremely concise essay
on *Adversity* in more ample form.   The ends
of the undeveloped paragraphs may be dis-
cerned at lines 8, 26, 38.

[1] No reference is to be understood here to the actual
process of composition.

II. THE PARAGRAPH.

A. The Paragraph Considered as an Undivided Whole.

10. The paragraph being already defined in its main relation, there remains only the application to it of those fundamental principles that govern the whole composition. A paragraph has unity when it can be summed up readily in a single sentence. In many paragraphs such a sentence appears at the beginning, or at the end, or in both places; but unity requires only that the reader should be able to sum up, not necessarily that the writer should sum up for him. Note which paragraphs, quoted in the following pages, state their themes, and which merely imply them.

11. The material proper to the development of a paragraph within the limits of unity is set forth by Professor Genung[1] in the following table for a typical paragraph:

[1] *Practical Elements of Rhetoric*, page 199. Professor Genung adds: "Of course this scheme is too

The subject proposed :

I. Whatever is needed to explain the subject.
    Repetition.
    Obverse (*i.e.*, presenting the contrary).
    Definition.

II. Whatever is needed to establish the subject.
    Exemplification or detail.
    Illustration.
    Proof.

III. Whatever is needed to apply the subject.
    Result or consequence.
    Enforcement.
    Summary or recapitulation.

In the paragraph next quoted point out these elements.

12. Coherence in a paragraph demands (1) a logical sequence of sentences, (2) usually the indication of this sequence by words of explicit reference. In the following para-

extensive for any particular paragraph; it merely represents the natural place for each manner of treatment adopted. Some parts may be condensed or altogether elided, others expanded so as to take up a prominent, even predominating proportion of the paragraph."

graph the words of explicit reference are
printed in italics.

First, the people of the colonies are descendants of Englishmen. *England*, Sir, is a nation
which still I hope respects, and formerly adored,
her freedom. The colonists emigrated from
you when *this* part of your character was most 5
predominant; and they took this bias and direction the moment they parted from your hands.
They are *therefore* not only devoted to liberty,
but to liberty according to English ideas, and
on English principles. Abstract *liberty*, like 10
other mere abstractions, is not to be found.
Liberty inheres in some sensible object; and
every nation has formed to itself some favorite
point, which by way of eminence becomes the
criterion of their happiness. It happened, you 15
know, Sir, that the great contests for freedom
in this country were from the earliest times
chiefly upon the question of taxing. Most of the
contests in the ancient commonwealths turned
primarily on the right of election of magis- 20
trates, or on the balance among the several
orders of the State. The question of money
was not with them so immediate. *But* in England it was otherwise. On *this point of taxes*
the ablest pens and most eloquent tongues have 25

been exercised; the greatest spirits have acted and suffered.   In order to give the fullest satisfaction concerning the importance of *this* point, it was not only necessary for those who in
30 argument defended the excellence of the English Constitution to insist on this privilege of granting money as a dry point of fact, and to prove that the right had been acknowledged in ancient parchments and blind usages to reside
35 in a certain body called a House of Commons. They went much *further;* they attempted to prove, and they succeeded, that in theory it ought to be so, from the particular nature of a House of Commons as an immediate represent-
40 ative of the people, whether the old records had delivered this oracle or not. They took infinite pains to inculcate, as a fundamental principle, that in all monarchies the people must in effect themselves, mediately or imme-
45 diately, possess the power of granting their own money, or no shadow of liberty could subsist.   The colonies draw from you, as with their life-blood, *these* ideas and principles. Their love of liberty, as with you, fixed and
50 attached on *this specific point of taxing. Liberty* might be safe, or might be endangered, in twenty other particulars, without their being much pleased or alarmed. *Here* they felt its

pulse; and as they found that beat, they thought themselves sick or sound. I do not 55 say whether they were right or wrong in applying your general arguments to their own case. It is not easy indeed to make a monopoly of theorems and corollaries. The fact is, that they did *thus* apply those general 60 arguments; and your mode of governing them, whether through lenity or indolence, through wisdom or mistake, confirmed them in the imagination, that they, as well as you, had an interest in these common principles.— 65 *Burke: On Conciliation with America.*

13. On analysis, the logical connection appears to be indicated mainly in three ways : (*a*) by conjunctions, etc.; (*b*) by demonstratives ; (*c*) by repetition of important words. With so great a range of choice the student is inexcusable who confines himself to perpetual *and* and *but.* For though Burke's nicety of adjustment is a distinguishing mark of his mastery, some care in adjustment must be taken from the beginning, or there will be small progress in composition. Examine also the following paragraph, and compare § 22.

The situation here contemplated exposes a
dreadful ulcer, lurking far down in the depths
of human nature.   It is not that men generally
are summoned to face such awful trials ; but
5 potentially, and in shadowy outline, such a
trial is moving subterraneously in perhaps all
men's natures.   Upon the secret mirror of
our dreams such a trial is darkly projected,
perhaps, to every one of us.   That dream, so
10 familiar to childhood, of meeting a lion, and,
through languishing prostration in hope and
the energies of hope, that constant sequel of
lying down before the lion, publishes the secret
frailty of human nature—reveals its •deep-
15 seated falsehood to itself—records its abysmal
treachery.   Perhaps not one of us escapes that
dream ; perhaps, as by some sorrowful doom
of man, that dream repeats for every one of
us, through every generation, the original
20 temptation in Eden.   Every one of us, in this
dream, has a bait offered to the infirm places
of his own individual will ; once again a snare
is presented for tempting him into captivity to
a luxury of ruin ; once again, as in aboriginal
25 Paradise, the man falls by his own choice ;
again, by infinite iteration, the ancient earth
groans to heaven, through her secret caves,
over the weakness of her child : " Nature, from

her seat, sighing through all her works," again
"gives signs of woe that all is lost ;" and again 30
the counter sigh is repeated to the sorrowing
heavens for the endless rebellion against God.
It is not without probability that in the world
of dreams every one of us ratifies for himself
the original transgression. In dreams, per- 35
haps under some secret conflict of the midnight
sleeper, lighted up to the consciousness at the
time, but darkened to the memory as soon as
all is finished, each several child of our myste-
rious race completes for himself the treason of 40
the aboriginal fall.—*De Quincey : The English
Mail-Coach.*

14. But observe that by no means all the
sentences in the paragraph at § 12 have
explicit reference, that some stand in *asyndeton.* Moreover, many of these sentences are
not less closely connected than the others.
Connection they have, but not connectives.
Examination will show here the rule that
asyndeton occurs : (*a*) when the succeeding
sentence is an expansion, iteration, example,
or illustration of the preceding—in other
words, when the connection is obvious ; (*b*)
2

when, as at line 15, a slight break is intended to mark a wider transition.   (Compare § 4.)

15. In the following paragraph, which has asyndeton throughout, observe the effect of abruptness.

But now, on the new system of travelling, iron tubes and boilers have disconnected man's heart from the ministers of his locomotion. Nile nor Trafalgar has power to raise an extra
5 bubble in a steam-kettle.   The galvanic cycle is broken up for ever; man's imperial nature no longer sends itself forward through the electric sensibility of the horse ; the inter-agencies are gone in the mode of communication
10 between the horse and his master, out of which grew so many aspects of sublimity under accidents of mists that hid, or sudden blazes that revealed, of mobs that agitated, or midnight solitudes that awed.   Tidings, fitted to con-
15 vulse all nations, must henceforwards travel by culinary process ; and the trumpet that once announced from afar the laurelled mail, heart-shaking when heard screaming on the wind, and proclaiming itself through the darkness to
20 every village or solitary house on its route, has now given way for ever to the pot-wallopings

of the boiler.—*De Quincey: The English Mail-Coach.*

Compare also the second example in § 19.

In revising for coherence, then, look first to the sequence of sentences, then to the indications of that sequence ; and, except in the cases noted above, or in the rare cases where abruptness is desired, avoid asyndeton.

16. The principles of emphasis as stated in §§ 5-7 apply without modification to the paragraph. Of the emphasis secured by prominence of position Bacon furnishes a more striking instance in the opening paragraph of his essay on *Ceremonies and Respects :*

He that is only real had need have exceeding great parts of virtue, as the stone had need to be rich that is set without foil. But if a man mark it well, it is in praise and commendation of men as it is in gettings and gains. For the proverb is true that light gains make heavy purses ; for light gains come thick, whereas great come but now and then. So it is true that small matters win great commendation, because they are continually in use and note, whereas the occasion of any great virtue cometh but on festivals. Therefore it doth much add to a man's reputation, and is, as Queen Isabella said, like perpetual letters commendatory, to have good forms.

17. Of the emphasis gained by proper proportion of space an admirable example is the paragraph quoted in § 12. The proposition developed by this paragraph may be stated as follows : *Since the American colonists are descendants of Englishmen, their love of liberty is fixed on this specific point of taxing.* The part concerning English descent, being subsidiary, is compressed within ten lines : the part concerning taxation, being the main point, occupies practically all the rest of the paragraph, fifty-five lines. The last sentence, though summing up only this latter part, is skilfully made to close with a reminder ("these *common* principles ") of the former.[1]

[1] Professor Wendell's formula for paragraph emphasis is useful, but too rigid : " A paragraph whose unity can be demonstrated by summarizing its substance in a sentence whose subject shall be a summary of its opening sentence, and whose predicate shall be a summary of its closing sentence, is theoretically well massed."—*English Composition*, page 129.

18. A particular means of paragraph emphasis is parallel construction, the balancing of sentence against sentence. It is most natural in successive expansions or iterations, or in an oratorical cumulation like the following:

Carry the principle on by which you expelled Mr. Wilkes, there is not a man in the House, hardly a man in the nation, who may not be disqualified. That this House should have no power of expulsion is a hard saying. That this House should have a general discretionary power of disqualification is a dangerous saying. That the people should not choose their own representative is a saying that shakes the constitution. That this House should name the representative is a saying which, followed by practice, subverts the constitution.—*Burke: Speech on the Middlesex Election.*

This last means of emphasis is somewhat too artificial to be commonly available. On the other hand, the first means, a strong close, is practically always useful ; and the second, due proportion of space, is obligatory.

B. The Paragraph Considered as a Series of Sentences.

19. A paragraph is commonly defined as a group of sentences with unity of purpose ; and though a paragraph is not primarily a group of sentences, yet ultimately it must be considered in this aspect. " In how many sentences shall this paragraph be developed ? " is a question, not merely of the extent, but also of the manner of development. Compare the two following paragraphs :

For my religion, though there be several circumstances that might persuade the world I have none at all, as the general scandal of my profession, the natural course of my studies,
5 the indifferency of my behaviour and discourse in matters of religion,—neither violently defending one, nor with that common ardour and contention opposing another—yet in despite hereof, I dare, without usurpation, as-
10 sume the honourable style of a Christian. Not that I merely owe this title to the font, my education, or the clime wherein I was born, as being bred up either to confirm those princi-

ples my parents instilled into my unwary un-
derstanding, or by a general consent proceed 15
in the religion of my country : but having in
my riper years and confirmed judgment seen
and examined all, I find myself obliged, by the
principles of grace, and the law of mine own
reason, to embrace no other name but this. 20
Neither doth herein my zeal so far make me
forget the general charity I owe unto human-
ity, as rather to hate than pity Turks, infi-
dels, and (what is worse) Jews ; rather con-
tenting myself to enjoy that happy style, than 25
maligning those who refuse so glorious a title.
Sir Thomas Browne: Religio Medici.

What is the hardest task in the world ? To
think. I would put myself in the attitude
to look in the eye an abstract truth, and I
cannot. I blench and withdraw on this side
and on that. I seem to know what he meant 5
who said, No man can see God face to face and
live. For example, a man explores the basis
of civil government. Let him intend his mind
without respite, without rest, in one direction.
His best heed long time avails him nothing. 10
Yet thoughts are flitting before him. We all but
apprehend, we dimly forebode the truth. We
say, I will walk abroad, and the truth will take

form and clearness to me. We go forth, but 15 cannot find it. It seems as if we needed only the stillness and composed attitude of the library to seize the thought. But we come in, and are as far from it as at first. Then, in a moment, and unannounced, the truth appears. 20 A certain wandering light appears, and is the distinction, the principle, we wanted. But the oracle comes because we had previously laid siege to the shrine. It seems as if the law of the intellect resembled that law of nature 25 by which we now inspire, now expire the breath; by which the heart now draws in, then hurls out the blood,—the law of undulation. So you must labor with your brains, and now you must forbear your activity and see 30 what the great Soul showeth. *Emerson: Intellect.*[1]

20. Apparently the question is "Long sentences or short?" And the answer is twofold. First, as a matter of logic, a given statement is left as an independent sentence or is combined in the same sentence with other statements according as it is coördinate or

[1] Quoted in Carpenter's *Exercises in Rhetoric and English Composition* in this connection.

subordinate. Logically, then, the question becomes : " Should this statement receive the prominence of a separate sentence, or should it be reduced to a clause or a phrase ? "[1] Here also is involved the principle of emphasis.

21. In the second place, as a matter of rhetoric, the succession of sentences in the first paragraph is smooth, in the second paragraph abrupt. And the difference, though it lies partly in explicit reference, lies mainly in the predominance of long or of short sentences. A paragraph of long sentences, then, has the advantage over a paragraph of short sentences in a nicer subordination and an easier flow. But it will not do to think of a paragraph as limited to one or the other. Each has its purpose, and both are necessary to variety. Moreover, since monotony of style means monotony in sentence-forms, variety in length is an end in itself.

22. Again, it is evident from §§ 12–15 that a paragraph is a group of sentences

---

[1] Practice in reduction of this kind is a direct means of overcoming a habit of redundancies.

when we consider its coherence. But para-graph coherence affects even the form of the sentences, by what has been called "inver-sion for adjustment."   A striking example of this is the following oratorical paragraph :

But the age of chivalry is gone.   That of soph-isters, œconomists, and calculators, has suc-ceeded ; and the glory of Europe is extinguished for ever.   Never, never more, shall we behold that generous loyalty to rank and sex, that proud submission, that dignified obedience, that sub-ordination of the heart, which kept alive, even in servitude itself, the spirit of an exalted freedom. The unbought grace of life, the cheap defence of nations, the nurse of manly sentiment and heroic enterprise, is gone ! It is gone, that sensibility of principle, that chastity of honour, which felt a stain like a wound, which inspired courage whilst it mitigated ferocity, which ennobled whatever it touched, and under which vice itself lost half its evil, by losing all its grossness.—*Burke : Reflec-tions on the Revolution in France.*

It should be added, first, that such inver-sions, besides contributing to paragraph co-herence, contribute also, like the exclamatory and interrogative forms, to emphasis and variety ; secondly, that inversion, exclamation, interrogation, all three must be regarded as exceptional. The frequent use of these devices makes style laboured and pompous.

The length of a sentence, then, and its form are to be decided, not absolutely for the sentence itself, but relatively to the paragraph.

III. THE SENTENCE.

23. In English every statement is punctu-
ated as a sentence unless it be definitely
subordinated to some other statement as a
dependent clause, or coördinated as an equal
member.   It is a common error to write— ⌣/

The tide was rising, so we ran.

Those seven words make two sentences—

The tide was rising.   So we ran.

For the two statements are left independent,
side by side.   Not punctuation, but only a
definite subordination will make them one
sentence—

We ran because the tide was rising ;

or, better,.

Since the tide was rising, we ran.

It is a grosser error to punctuate a clause
as if it were a sentence.   Until these two con-

verse errors are eradicated, nothing further can be done. No one can revise for sentence unity until he recognizes the unit.

24. Except in that it is easier to unify a short sentence than a long one, the length of a sentence has nothing to do with its unity. Above are seven words not in unity, and at lines 27–35 in the paragraph at § 12 are seventy words entirely in unity. Besides, the length of a sentence depends, partly upon the exigencies of the individual thought, partly upon the emphasis of the whole paragraph (§ 20). Length, then, is not the test, but relevance, the bearing of the modifiers on the main part. In the following sentence the modifiers move steadily away from the main part :

In this uneasy state Cicero was oppressed by a new and cruel affliction, the death of his daughter Tullia, which happened soon after her divorce from Dolabella, whose manners and humours were entirely disagreeable to her.

The remedy here is simple. Cast out the irrelevant modifiers. If they are not worthy the dignity of separate sentences, suppress them altogether. In general, beware of the-House-that-Jack-built sentence.

25. But the trouble is deeper. Wherein lies the absurdity of the following sentence ?

I turned to reply, when the platform on which I was standing gave way with a crash.

Here the writer unintentionally represents himself as unmoved in the midst of disaster :

When the platform on which I was standing gave way with a crash, I turned to reply.

The sentence is logically upside down, the main thought being expressed as subordinate, the subordinate thought as main. This corrected, the sentence is at once logical.

When I turned to reply, the platform on which I was standing gave way with a crash.

The following sentence has the same fault, but the remedy is to cut the sentence in two :

Vasco de Gama first doubled Cape Colony, and later, in 1652, the Dutch came and made settlements there, when England, always anxious for new territory, seized all South Africa, with the attending results of six wars with the natives and with a mixture of natives and Dutch settlers.

In a word, a complex sentence must have only one main part, and that part must be expressed as the main clause.

26. In compound sentences, where there is no one main part, unity demands that there shall be real coördination, that the members shall be co-equal parts of one main idea. Unity appears in the balanced sentences at § 40. Most of the compound sentences that violate unity, except such as make merely irrelevant additions with *and*, do so because they violate coherence (§ 28).

In revising sentences for unity, then :

(1) See that the punctuation tells the truth.

(2) See that the main thought is in the main clause, not in some modifier.

(3) See that the modifiers are relevant.

(4) See that the members of compound sentences are really coördinate parts of one idea.

27. Coherence in a sentence is primarily correctness in syntax, and, as such, is hardly matter of rhetoric. Almost all solecisms are but forms of what the Greeks called *anacoluthon*. Thus *different than* puts a conjunction after a word logically followed by a preposition ; thus the so-called hanging participle [1] is a construction left unfinished ; thus *and which* [2] tries to make a clause at once coördinate and subordinate ; and so of faults in correlation [3] and in the sequence of tenses. [4]

28. But coherence in a sentence is also

---

[1] " Coming nearer, the shores were seen to be wooded."

[2] The combination *and which* is correct only when *which*-clauses are coördinated, as in the last sentence of the paragraph quoted at § 22.

[3] The rule for correlatives (*either-or*, *neither-nor*, *rather than*, *partly-partly*, etc., etc.) is that they should stand in positions absolutely corresponding, each to each (compare § 32, b, c). The error is the slipshod " Neither by sea nor land."

[4] *e.g.*, " He intended to have gone," for " He intended to go." Professor Genung states the rule thus : " In dependent clauses and infinitives the tense is to be counted relatively to the principal assertion, not absolutely in itself."—*Practical Elements of Rhetoric*, page 112.

matter of logic. The legend in open electric cars—

Avoid danger. Keep your seats till the car stops,

or

Avoid danger and keep your seats, etc.,

is illogical. The error of the former will appear on reference to § 20. Substantially the same is the error of the latter. The writer has made two requests where he meant to make one. He has written as coördinate a clause that is clearly subordinate. He means—

To avoid danger, keep your seats, etc.

The connecting thus by the coördinating conjunction *and* or *but* of two statements that are not coördinate is one of the commonest, as it is one of the gravest, phases of incoherence. The remedy is to be found not so much in the avoidance of *and* and *but* as in educating oneself to distinguish readily what is subordinate from what is coördinate. In brief, avoid illogical compound sentences.

3

29. Thus unity and coherence unite in demanding that the sentence adhere throughout to one plan.   But, furthermore, that plan must at every point be clear.   Failure in this may almost always be traced to one of three kinds of error : (a) undue ellipsis, (b) faulty reference, (c) faulty placing of modifiers.

(a) undue ellipsis.

Cardinal Richelieu hated Buckingham as sincerely as the Spaniard Olivares (ellipsis of the verb).

Daudet is nearer Trollope than Dickens (ellipsis of the preposition).

Even to-day many people are found who could not be induced to sit down in a party of thirteen at table, in the dread that one of the number would die within a short time, or would surely faint if a white cat were to enter the house (ellipsis of the relative).

(b) faulty reference.

If a man has done an Indian a wrong his only safety lies in killing him (ambiguity of personal pronouns).

So on the third day he rode over a long bridge,

and there started upon him a passing foul churl, and he smote his horse on the nose so that he turned about and asked him why he rode over that bridge without his license [ambiguity of personal pronouns. Compare (c)].

Black Death was the name given to an Oriental plague marked by inflammatory boils which in the fourteenth century desolated the world [ambiguity of the relative pronoun. Compare (c)].

(c) faulty placing of modifiers.

They are separated from the class to which they belonged *in consequence of their crimes.*

Though we are all *by no means* connoisseurs, yet we all go to exhibitions, not because it is the fashion, but because we think it elevates our minds.

In this chapter is seen the master of Thornfield led about like a child *crushed in attempting to save his wife* who perished in the flames she had created.

30. Blunders of these types have given rise to the following cautions :

(1) A given pronoun must refer throughout a given sentence exclusively and unmistakably to one antecedent.

(2) The position of any modifier should be next to the word it modifies, or as near as possible. Negatives and the words *only*, *merely*, *hardly*, etc., demand especial attention.

(3) Non-restrictive ("coördinate") relative clauses are always set off by commas, restrictive clauses never.[1]

31. The unity and coherence of a sentence being properly matters of grammar, under emphasis is included all that may strictly be called the rhetoric of the sentence, the rules, that is, of effective form. For most effective sentence-forms are applications of the rule (§§ 5–6) concerning prominence of position. Of all such forms two stand as types, the *period* and the *climax*. A third, the *balance*, though not logically distinct from the two former, is so marked as to deserve separate treatment. None of these terms, in fact, is

---

[1] It is a practice with some careful writers to accentuate this distinction by confining *who* and *which*, so far as is possible, to non-restrictive clauses; *i.e.*, by using *that* always for restrictive clauses. Though this practice may not be insisted on, it is undoubtedly useful.

exclusive of the others; but each marks a model of construction.

32. *The periodic sentence, or period*, keeps its construction incomplete up to the end. It closes grammatically with the last word, not before. All sentences that are not periodic are technically called *loose*. In general, that suspension of the sense which is characteristic of the period is accomplished (a) by putting all the modifiers before the main part, or (b) by the use of correlatives and other words of suspense, or (c) by a combination of these methods.

(a)

Apart from such an assertion, or such a result, I myself am little aware of the pace.—*De Quincey: The English Mail-Coach.*

Such now being at that time the usages of mail-coaches, what was to be done by us of young Oxford ?—*ibid.*

Many a stern republican, after gorging himself with a full feast of admiration of the Grecian commonwealths and of our true Saxon constitution, and discharging all the splendid bile of his virtuous indignation on King John and King James, sits down perfectly satisfied to the coarsest work and homeliest job of the day he lives in.—*Burke : Thoughts on the Present Discontents.*

An influence which operated without noise and without violence ; an influence which converted the very antagonist into the instrument of power ; which contained in itself a perpetual principle of growth and renovation ; and which the distresses and the prosperity of the country equally tended to augment, was an admirable substitute for a prerogative that, being only the offspring of anti- quated prejudices, had moulded in its original stamina irresistible principles of decay and disso- lution.—*ibid.*

Compare the first sentence in the paragraph quoted at § 19.

(b), (c)

This doctrine, as applied to the prince now on the British throne, *either* is nonsense, and there- fore neither true nor false, *or* it affirms a most unfounded, dangerous, illegal, and unconstitu- tional position.—*Burke : Reflections on the Rev- olution in France.*

Yet have I not *so* shaken hands with those des- perate resolutions who had rather venture at large their decayed bottom, than bring her in to be new trimmed at the dock, who had rather promiscuously retain all, than abridge any, and obstinately be what they are, than what they have been, *as* to stand in diameter and swords' point with them.—*Sir Thomas Browne: Religio Medici.*

The little cany carriage—*partly*, perhaps, from the violent torsion of the wheels in its recent movement, *partly* from the the thundering blow we had given to it—as if it sympathized with human horror, was all alive with tremblings and shiverings.—*De Quincey: The English Mail-Coach.*

Some twenty or more years before I matriculated at Oxford, Mr. Palmer, at that time M.P. for Bath, had accomplished *two* things, very hard to do on our little planet the Earth, however cheap they may be held by eccentric people in comets—he had invented mail-coaches, and he had married the daughter of a duke.—*ibid.*

Among them, *indeed*, I saw some of known rank, some of shining talents ; but of any practical experience in the state, not one man was to be found.—*Burke : Reflections on the Revolution in France.*

33. The main characteristics of this periodic form are four :

(1) It is more formal than the loose sentence.

(2) It tends toward unity, the suspense tending to force out irrelevant modifiers.

(3) It tends toward coherence.

(4) It is decidedly emphatic, both because the main part comes at the close and because the suspense stimulates the mind to receive the close with attention. Naturally, therefore, it has been a favourite form with all great orators. Moreover, Herbert Spencer[1] explicitly maintains that by presenting the whole idea at once to the mind, instead of building it up bit by bit as the loose sentence does, the period secures the greatest economy of attention.

34. In all these respects, except the single one of formality, the loose sentence seems inferior. But formality is hardly to be sought, and most certainly to be sought is variety (§ 21). Therefore no one is free to use the period exclusively, even if he would. Be-

[1] *Philosophy of Style*, pages 20–22 (American edition).

sides, the term *loose sentence*, being so much more inclusive than the term *period*, being in fact only a negative, needs further elucidation.

We frequently hear the habit of reading lauded highly and the acquiring of it recommended, to the young in particular, usually in very general terms, as if its advantages were truths so self-evident that no one would think of denying them, very much indeed as we hear religion praised, or industry, no matter to what applied, or any other of what are considered the safeguards of society.

The weakness of this loose sentence lies in the fact that it sounds, in great part, like a succession of after-thoughts. Instead of receiving a definitely formulated idea, the reader feels as if he were called on to assist at the process of formulation. The successive modifiers call for successive revisions of the original statement. Few styles are more tiresome or more irritating than one in which such sentences are habitual.

He sent a life of Milton to the Edinburgh Review, and contributed several articles to that magazine up to the time he entered Parliament, where he made himself immediately famous as an orator.

This loose sentence violates emphasis by violating unity.

In western cities the theatres are open on Sunday, but in New York Sunday entertainments of that class are confined principally to so-called sacred concerts, although it is doubtful what selections that are played could be rightly termed sacred music.

Here the writer evidently has not even decided which is his main idea.

35. All three loose sentences above violate the principle of emphasis ; all are typical of the danger of the loose sentence, the danger of mere aggregation. But in the following loose sentence the principle of emphasis is just as evidently observed as in the period :

In such a people the haughtiness of domination combines with the spirit of freedom, fortifies it, and renders it invincible.—*Burke : On Conciliation with America.*

Equally emphatic are the loose sentences in the paragraph quoted from the same author at § 22. Sentences in which, as in these, the parts succeed in ascending scale are said to have *climax*.

36. Climax, moreover, does not mean merely that the succeeding clauses have stronger and stronger words. The climax in the following is gained by such successive expansions of the thought as make it grow in significance while one reads :

Such preeminently is Shakespeare among ourselves; such preeminently Virgil among the Latins ; such in their degree are all those writers who in every nation go by the name of Classics.— *Newman : Literature.*

A sentence has climax when there is a logical advance from clause to clause up to the point of the sentence. Both the following sentences exemplify this, and at the same time, by the way in which the first leads up to the second, show how sentence emphasis is involved in paragraph coherence (§ 22).

And what that energy, which is the life of genius, above everything demands and insists upon, is freedom ; entire independence of all authority, prescription, and routine,—the fullest room to expand as it will.   Therefore, a nation whose chief spiritual characteristic is energy, will not be very apt to set up, in intellectual matters, a fixed standard, an authority, like an academy.—*Matthew Arnold: The Literary Influence of Academies.*

37. " Period or loose sentence ? " then, in so far as the question concerns the single sentence, not the whole paragraph, should be answered with an eye to certain maxims :

(1) Either form may be good or bad.

(2) The period is more stimulating to closeness of thought, in the reader and in the writer.

(3) A short period is more commonly useful than a long one.   The short period, in fact, might be called the most useful of sentence-forms.

(4) The loose sentence has often a more direct, a more conversational effect.

(5) The loose sentence is emphatic in proportion as it has climax.

38. So far only one position of emphasis has been considered, the end. The beginning is also emphatic, but not in the same degree as the beginning of a paragraph. For the fact that most English sentences, on account of the lack of inflections in English and the consequent dependence of clearness upon the order of words (§ 29, c), begin with the subject, detracts somewhat from the emphasis of the subject in this position. Conversely, some other part of the sentence, not so naturally expected in that position, receives emphasis at the beginning :

At Sens, thirty miles away to the west, a place of far graver aspect, the name of Jean Cousin denotes a more chastened temper, even in these sumptuous decorations.—*Pater : Imaginary Portraits.*

39. Observe also that additional emphasis is thrown upon the opening phrase of the sentence above by the break that follows. Even the subject may be emphasized in this position by a following parenthesis :

The Cecils, we suspect, did their best to spread

this opinion by whispers and insinuations.—*Macaulay : Francis Bacon.*

Strangers, meanwhile, were less unjust to the young barrister than his nearest kinsman had been.—*ibid.*

It should be remembered, however, that the beginning of any sentence, more than any other part of it, is subject to the paragraph.

40. The term *balance*, as applied to sentences, is self-defining (compare § 18). Balance to a certain extent is required of all sentences (§ 27). In all ordinary collocations symmetry has been made a part of correctness. Lapses in this jar upon the ear. And such sentences as the following, though they cannot be called incorrect, have the same effect of discord :

The Roman Catholic goes to mass and devotes the rest of the day to pleasure, while the Protestant goes to church and rests the remainder of the day.

One feels that the two contrasted statements should be alike in form, that in form as in substance they should be halves of one whole. Developed more highly, this desire for balance has led to many memorable sentences :

When his imagination wells up, it overflows in ornament ; when his heart is touched, it thrills along his verse.—*Newman : Literature.*

The power of French literature is in its prose writers ; the power of English literature is in its poets.—*Matthew Arnold : The Literary Influence of Academies.*

41. Here the sentence is cast in halves. This, technically speaking, is the balanced sentence, as distinguished from such sentences as contain balance incidentally. Where the effect of correspondence is heightened by repetition, the balance approaches epigram :

The party whose principles afforded him no guarantee would be attached to him by interest : the party whose interests he attacked would be restrained from insurrection by principle.—*Macaulay : History of England.*

To make us love our country, our country ought to be lovely.—*Burke : Reflections on the Revolution in France.*

It was dangerous to trust the sincerity of Augustus : to seem to distrust it was still more dangerous.—*Gibbon : Decline and Fall of the Roman Empire.*

42. The last example has the inverted balance called by the Greeks *chiasmus.* It is hardly necessary to point out that the English sentence is not flexible to such forms. Even simple balance easily conveys in English an impression of artificiality hardly felt in the more flexible Greek and Latin. For this reason, and on account of the obvious monotony of a series of balanced sentences, the form has in English a limited use. But, though limited, its use is very distinct and very great. Pithy summaries, especially such as approach epigram, are much heightened by the balance ; and, in general, it is an admirable mould for emphatic compound sentences.

INDEX TO THE SECTIONS

4

INDEX TO THE EXTRACTS

(NOTE. *Punctuation and capitals have in some cases been modified in the direction of uniformity.*)